*happiness is ...*
快樂就是……

# happiness is ...

## 500 ways to be in the moment

# 快樂就是……

## 500個值得珍惜的當下日常

### 《快樂就是……》第2集

麗莎・史瓦琳 & 拉夫・羅拉薩
Lisa Swerling & Ralph Lazar

taking the road less traveled
踏上一條少有人跡的路

reading a book that's set in
the place you're traveling
在旅途中，讀一本以當地為主題的書

seeing someone cry from
really good news

見到有人因為聽見天大的好
消息而流下快樂的眼淚

catching a rainbow in a prism

從三稜鏡裡，看見一道彩虹

folding warm laundry

把剛洗完、烘好的衣服折起來。暖暖的

going right back to sleep
after waking up in the
middle of the night

半夜醒來之後，
又馬上睡著

tuning out distractions
把讓自己分心的人與事都從腦中趕走

just sitting and thinking
就只是坐著，想著

when your dog
licks your ear
小狗狗跑來舔你的耳朵

forgiving a friend
原諒朋友

a good scalp massage
有人幫你好好的按摩頭皮

letting go of negative thoughts
放下了負面的想法

sketching in an
art gallery

在美術館裡畫畫

giving a gift for no
reason in particular

送一份禮物給朋友，不必有理由

walking in deep snow
走在深深、鬆鬆的雪裡

filling and burying a time capsule

做一個時空膠囊，然後埋起來

writing down daily intentions
寫下每天想做的事

making your own
delicious-smelling soaps
自己煮一鍋好香好香的湯

15

taking in the view
from a bridge
在橋上欣賞美景

reading the newspaper
cover to cover

拿一份報紙，好整以暇地從
第一個字讀到最後一個字

a child mumbling in their sleep

聽見孩子在睡夢中咕噥著

*cooking with love*
懷著愛，為所愛的人做飯

*refusing to let anyone steal your joy*
不讓別人偷偷帶走自己的快樂

flannel pajamas on the first
cold night of the year
在今年變冷的第一個晚上，穿著柔軟的法藍絨睡衣

jumping on hotel beds
在旅館的大床上盡情跳啊跳

feeling the wind in your hair
感覺風吹動了我頭髮

the smell of spring
聞到春天的味道

a windowsill of
beautiful succulents

窗台上擺滿了漂亮的仙人掌

the quiet calm of a bookshop

書店裡靜謐的氣氛

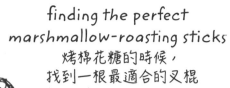

finding the perfect
marshmallow-roasting sticks
烤棉花糖的時候，
找到一根最適合的叉棍

the smell of lavender
薰衣草的香味

reliving childhood games
和小朋友一起玩遊戲，回憶童年

exploring
new places
探索新的地方

writing a letter to
someone instead of
sending an e-mail
不寄電郵，而是親手
寫一封信給朋友

sleeping when the
baby sleeps
趁著小嬰孩睡著的空檔，
自己打個盹

goofing around
with friends
和朋友鬼混消磨時間

feeling beautiful from within
發自內心感到自己很美

好預兆

*having a good sigh
every now and then*
經常有好的預感

*overcoming fears*
克服了恐懼

letting the emotions flow
允許自己表露出情緒

sharing homegrown
veggies
拿自家栽種的蔬菜
和朋友分享

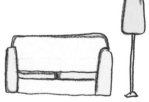

cleaning to calm your inner chaos
心裡煩躁的時候，打掃家裡，讓自己平緩下來

feeling inspired to write before going to bed
睡前突然有書寫的靈感

seeing the bulbs you planted in autumn bloom in spring
春天時，看見去年秋天種下的種子發芽了

sailing on a sunny day
大晴天揚帆出航

being the bigger
person in a conflict
吵贏人家，爽啦

chasing a butterfly
追著蝴蝶跑

accepting the world as it is
順其自然，就這樣子吧

exchanging handwritten
letters with a friend
和朋友互寄手寫的信札

tidying your sock drawer
把衣櫃裡的襪子整理好，
全部成雙成對

playing with little kids
和小朋友玩耍

*the way the air feels
before a storm*
暴風雨來臨之前，
空氣中的凝重感覺

*perfecting the noble
art of having fun*
努力精進「享樂」這個技藝

a bubble bath on
a weeknight
週間夜晚好好享受一個泡泡浴

*helping someone*
*without being asked*
不待詢問，主動幫助他人

*alone time with a*
*notebook and pen*
一支筆，一本筆記簿的
個人時光

*growing flowers in*
*the windowsill*
在窗台上種花

dancing and singing at
the top of your lungs

扯開喉嚨唱歌，一面跳舞

taking a whole day for
an activity you love

用一整天，做一件你最愛的事

a bunch of balloons
一大把氣球

making an
exceptional flower
arrangement

完成一個超讚的插花作品

thinking, dreaming, planning
想東想西…做著白日夢…
想著要做的事

a full moon hike
滿月之夜，出門健行

dreaming about the book
you're reading
夢到睡前在讀的那本書

wet, fresh-smelling hair
剛洗好頭髮，濕濕的，
香香的

a small child
singing to you
一個小朋友唱歌給你聽

a good stretch
好好伸展身體

spending a whole day
with your kids
一整天陪著孩子

going through a box of old letters and photos
瀏覽那些老照片還有信件

being yourself
做自己就好

running full speed into the water
全速衝進水裡

watching clouds
看著雲

*a good yoga class*
一堂令人舒暢的瑜珈課

taking the time to put
something together
properly
花時間把某樣東西正確地
組合起來

*running your worries away*

跑呀跑，直到憂慮都消失了

*making an elaborate
sandcastle*

堆出一座精緻的沙堡

a kiss on the
forehead
before bed
睡前在額頭上的一吻

watching the rain
slide off the roof
看著雨水流下屋簷

holding your mother's hand

牽媽媽的手

painting a long wooden fence

為一座木頭圍籬上漆

finishing all your paperwork

寫完報告了

losing track of time while
creating something

專心做著某事，都忘了時間

acting like children in public
在大庭廣眾之下表現得像個孩子

climbing under freshly cleaned sheets
鑽進剛洗好的被子

a road trip with friends
和好友一起開車出去玩

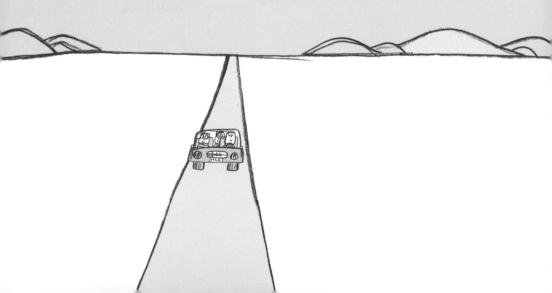

long talks with mom
和媽媽聊天，聊了好久

scented candles
香氛蠟燭的味道

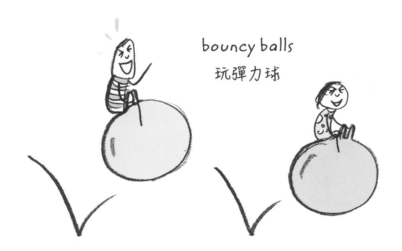

bouncy balls
玩彈力球

fresh-cut flowers
at work
上班的時候，聞到花香

relishing
accomplishments
好好回味自己的成就

playing around
with someone
you love
和你愛的人一起玩

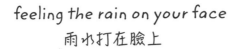

feeling the rain on your face
雨水打在臉上

not looking back
永不回頭

a cozy room with
twinkle lights

在舒服的房間裡，有一
閃一閃的燈光伴隨

*a perfect thinking spot*
一處可以獨自沈思的完美地點

a glass of wine at the
end of a long day
漫長的一天結束之際，
喝一杯酒

drawing a perfectly straight
line without a ruler
不用尺就畫出一條超完美直線

a no-boss-day
at work
今天老闆不進辦公室

having a friend who always
boosts your mood
一個永遠能夠提振你心情的朋友

a patch of wildflowers
一叢野花

hugging for no
reason at all
來個擁抱，無須理由

sitting back, relaxing,
and enjoying the flight
在座位上坐好，放輕鬆，
享受這趟飛行

living within your means
憑著自己的能力而活

*a super productive
day at work*
一個效率超高的工作日

*letting someone
spoil you*
任他／她寵我吧

*napping in the sunshine*
在暖暖的陽光下打瞌睡

waking up on a trip and
forgetting where you are

在旅途中醒來，忘了自己在哪

a wishing well
許願井

small gestures
一次小小的示好

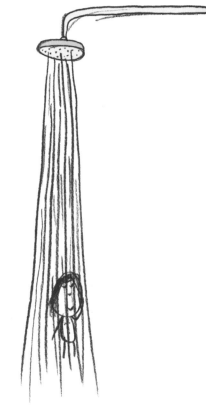

a hot shower with the
perfect water pressure
洗一個水量強勁的熱水澡

63

walking on
crunchy leaves
踩在枯葉上

when everyone appreciates the food you cooked
大家都喜歡你煮的菜

spending quality time
with friends
和朋友共度一段美好的時光

watching a downpour
看著傾盆大雨

*a summer water fight*
夏天打水仗

*lying on the sofa after a big meal*
大餐後整個人癱在沙發上

forgetting about the world
while playing your favorite
instrument

彈奏你最喜歡的樂器，
忘了整個世界

visiting your old school and
sharing memories

重訪母校，和朋友分享回憶

pausing for reflection

暫停腳步，思索一番

stopping by because you're
in the neighborhood
既然在附近了，就去拜訪朋友吧

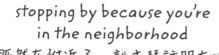

hugging good-bye but
not wanting to let go
擁抱著道別，很不想放手

coffee and a
long catch-up
喝著咖啡，好好聊聊近況

staring out the back window
從汽車後座望出去

believing
我相信！

由此去
更好

knowing that better times lie ahead
深信前路更美好

sharing a hobby
with friends
和一群志趣相合的朋友
在一起

decluttering
斷！捨！離！

leaving money in the meter for the next person
把停車計時器的餘額送給下一個車主

seeing your dog after a long time away
離家多日之後返家，與小狗重逢

getting new plants
買了新的盆栽

when a butterfly lands on you
一隻蝴蝶停在你手上

enough coffee
for two
咖啡足夠兩人享用

collecting firewood on a beach
在沙灘上蒐集柴薪

treating a friend to a meal
請好友吃飯

lending someone a book
you adored reading
把自己喜愛的好書借給人

the first sprouts of a new
garden
新花園裡長出新芽

packing for an adventure
收拾行李準備展開旅程

taking lunch away
from your desk
中午離開辦公室用餐

learning to read music
學著看樂譜

a bear hug from a child
小朋友給你一個熊抱

being curious
好奇心

saying sorry
道歉

letting go of things that make you feel bad,
and hanging on to those that make you feel good
放手讓負面的事遠離，留住正面的事

deep conversations over dinner
晚餐時做深度交談

admiring family photos
欣賞家族照片

letting a child do your hair
讓孩子幫你弄頭髮

being nice to people
和善待人

a family art project
全家一起創作

daydreaming
做白日夢

learning from life's teachers
向人生的導師學習

poring over a map
to plan an adventure
為了規劃旅遊而仔細
研究地圖

finding the
perfect name for
your new blog
為自己的部落格找到
最完美的名稱

morning
meditation
晨間冥想

a massage in a foreign land
人在外地做按摩

writing a letter using
multicolored pens
用好幾種顏色的筆
撰寫一封信

decorating a birthday cake
裝飾生日蛋糕

hunting for shells
摸蛤仔

new frontiers
探索未知之地

a promising message
in a fortune cookie
抽到上上籤

an outdoor shower
在野外洗澡

a big adventure
一場大冒險

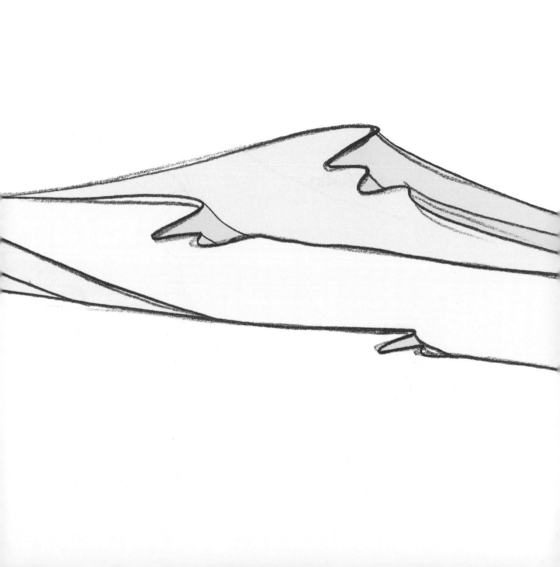

sweating out the stress
流汗舒壓

a kitty belly rub
撫弄貓咪的肚皮

hiding money in
someone's pocket
把錢偷偷塞進對方的
皮夾裡

rewatching your favorite movie
重看一次最愛的電影

the smell of your
mother's perfume
聞到媽媽的香水

breaking the top of
a crème brûlée
壓碎法式焦糖布蕾的脆皮

a long beach walk
一次長長的海灘漫步

playing in the pool
在泳池玩水

planting a community garden
在社區花園裡栽種

社區花園

an empty laundry basket
洗衣籃清空了

finally playing a piece
of music correctly
終於把一首樂曲彈對

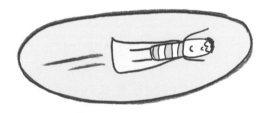

holding on to your dreams
不放棄夢想

jumping into a pile of leaves
跳進一堆枯葉

finding a secret
place to write
找到私房寫作地點

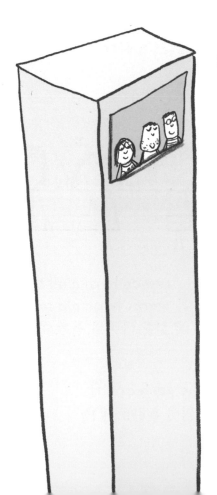

having friends over to
your new apartment
搬入新公寓之後請朋友來訪

cheering someone up
為別人打氣

having a serious
conversation in baby
language
和小嬰孩認真對話

remembering all the
words to an old song
完整記得一首老歌的歌詞

giving the perfect gift
送出一個對方喜歡的禮物

*climbing your favorite tree*
爬上你最愛的那棵大樹

drawing with your feet in the sand

用腳在沙灘上作畫

walking with a puppy
帶小狗散步

playing hide-and-seek
玩捉迷藏

hiking with someone
small on your back

背上背著小朋友，一起去健行

the first ladybug of spring
今年春天第一次見到瓢蟲

seeing an orchid
finally bloom
看到蘭花終於開了

when for some reason
everything feels just right
不知什麼原因，一切都是
這麼的順心

traveling to a new country by yourself
獨自去一個沒去過的國家

celebrating your birthday with friends
朋友為你慶生

dipping your nose into a bag of
freshly ground coffee
把鼻子湊近一袋剛磨好的咖啡豆聞聞看

cooking a fancy meal for yourself
為自己好好做一頓飯

*unpacking the last box in your new home*
搬入新家後，拆開最後一個箱子

*filling a whole journal*
寫完一整本日記

a smile creeping across
your face when a good
memory flutters by

因著一個美好的回憶掠過腦海，
使得臉上浮現了微笑

waking up to find
your child has
climbed into your bed

醒來發現孩子不知
何時爬上了你的床

110

dancing like the whole
world has disappeared
盡情跳舞，完全不管他人眼光

going with the flow
順著水流漂呀漂

taking compliments
from a stranger
接受陌生人的讚美

the smell of a fire in the fireplace
在火爐前，聞著柴火燃燒的味道

sneaking outside to enjoy a
morning cup of coffee
一個人溜到外面，
享受早上的咖啡

making your
own jewelry
自製首飾

baking a surprise batch
of cookies
烤一盤餅乾，給大家驚喜

writing the first line of
a new story
寫下一個新故事的開頭

making pickles
做泡菜

asking an older person to
share stories from their youth
請長輩把他年輕時的故事告訴你

staying the course

維持在預定的航道上

your kids running to meet
you when you get home
回家時，看到孩子跑來迎接你

designing your own house
設計自己的家

making funny films
with friends
和朋友拍攝爆笑視頻

getting the slow-cooker
on in the early afternoon

午後，開啟燉鍋做菜

shedding baggage and
traveling light

拋開不必要的行李，
一身輕便的去旅行

liking what you see
in the mirror
喜歡鏡子裡看到的自己

making a wish on
a dandelion
對著蒲公英許願

*a spontaneous picnic*

說走就走去野餐

breathing deeply
深呼吸

not checking e-mail
不要查看電郵信箱

savoring a perfect macchiato
細細品嚐一杯完美的瑪奇朵

sitting outside on a warm night
溫暖的夜晚，坐在門外

writing a song for someone
寫首歌獻給某人

embracing your alter ego
接受自己個性中的另一面

starting a big project
with a friend
和朋友合作一個
大計畫

planning a surprise party
規劃一個驚喜派對

chilling out to
mellow music
在輕柔的樂聲中
冷靜下來

unplugging from everything

暫時與外隔絕
摒除一切雜念

accepting people
for who they are
接受朋友們的本性

having friends who know
what's important
擁有一群志同道合的朋友

finishing a drawing
畫完一幅畫

expressing your unique sense of humor
表達你獨特的幽默感

taking a time-out
暫停一下

a yoga retreat

參加瑜珈營隊

watching birds from your window in the morning
早上看著窗外的鳥兒

exchanging smiles with an older person on the street
在街上與長輩互相微笑

feeling the sun
on your skin
讓太陽曬著肌膚

coming home to the smell
of your favorite dish
一回家就聞到自己最愛吃的菜的香味

homemade sodas
在家自製飲料

watching the tides
for hours
連續好幾個小時看著流水

improvised games
隨興想出的遊戲

having friends over to
watch an old movie
朋友來家裡一起欣賞老電影

growing your own herbs
in the kitchen
在廚房種植香料植物

exploring an old cellar
到古舊的地下室探險

when you blow out the candles in one breath
一口氣吹熄蠟燭

making a dish from your
mother's favorite recipe book
參看媽媽最喜歡的食譜，然後做出一道菜

letting your voice be heard

大聲說出來

long stories from
little people

小孩子口中說出的
長篇故事

sunshine after
days of rain

多日陰雨，終於放晴

*arranging flowers you
picked from your garden*
在院子採花，然後插起來

*calling your dad
just to say hi*
打電話給爸爸，只想說聲嗨

*mastering a new skill*
把一個新風箏飛起來

music that
perfectly describes
your mood

一首能完美表達你現在
心境的樂曲

blending fresh juices

現打鮮果汁

remembering that as one
door closes, another opens

熊熊想起，雖然關上了一扇門，
別處必定打開一扇新門

goofing around with dad
和爸爸嬉鬧

trying your best
despite hardship
縱使很困難，
也要全力以赴

chatting with your neighbor
和鄰居閒聊

working as a team
團隊一心合作

a book that changes your life

一本改變你生命的書

giving a shoulder rub,
just because
來個肩膀按摩，
不必問為什麼

being honest
with yourself
誠實面對自己

hot soup on a
chilly day
在冷天享受熱湯

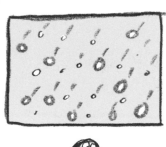

encouraging your
child's dreams
鼓勵孩子追求夢想

a sunrise excursion
一大早就出門遊玩

dozing off while
reading

讀著讀著，
就睡了

not caring what others think of you
別管別人怎麼想

a free day with nothing to do
空閒的日子，什麼事都沒有

catching your
first wave
首度衝浪成功！

cooking dinner over the fire
用營火煮晚餐

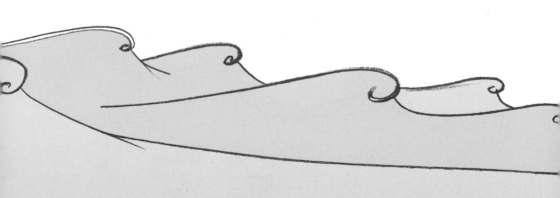

*a girls' weekend*
女孩的專屬週末

*seeing the moon from your bed*
躺在床上看見窗外的月亮

writing something you've already
done on your to-do list,
just to check it off
把完成的事情，
從待辦清單上面刪除

kissing often
經常親親

cooking a huge gourmet meal
烹調一頓精美大餐

flying tiny paper
planes
射紙飛機

a moment of inspiration
靈光乍現的時刻

slowing down
放慢速度

someone apologizing before
you have a chance to ask
你還沒提出要求，
他就先道歉了

designing your own dress
設計自己的洋裝

your first handstand
學會倒立

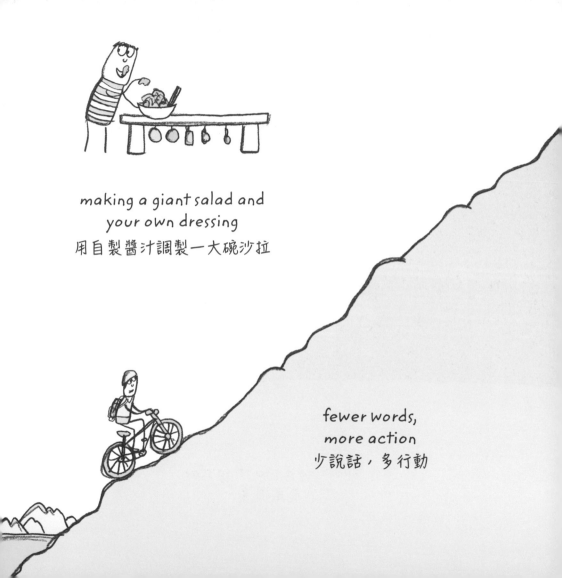

making a giant salad and
your own dressing
用自製醬汁調製一大碗沙拉

fewer words,
more action
少說話，多行動

spotting a shooting star
看見流星

*a family dinner of*
*spaghetti and meatballs*
全家人一起吃肉丸義大利麵

*fresh pajamas after a long bath*
洗完一個長長的澡，穿上新睡衣

making time for coffee after lunch
午餐過後，留點時間喝咖啡

being forgiving
寬以待人

playing a song
you wrote
彈奏自己創作的曲子

*a new haircut*
剛剪完頭髮

*the smell of baby powder*
爽身粉的香味

*letting your dog hang out the car window*
開車時讓狗狗把頭伸出窗外

writing a list of books you've
read in the last twelve months
寫下過去一年你讀過哪些書

having friends who feed you
朋友們請你吃東西

sweeping the front
walk with a really
good new broom

拿一把高品質的新掃把，
清掃門前

a smile
with dimples

微笑的時候
露出酒窩

making a baby giggle
把嬰孩逗得咯咯笑

a bird feeder in the yard
庭院裡擺一個餵鳥器

blowing bubbles
吹泡泡

coming home and
hopping straight into bed
一回家直接跳上床

walking barefoot
on wet grass
光腳踩在濕濕的草地上

helping someone who is lost
幫助迷路的人

making soup with vegetables
you grew yourself

用自家種的蔬菜煮湯

driving less, cycling more

少開車，多騎腳踏車

*rearranging your bookshelf
in alphabetical order*

按照字母順序，重新整理書架

the sense of being a kindred spirit
with someone you've just met

和某個剛認識的人很投緣

sharing your last piece
of chocolate

和人分享最後一塊巧克力

designing your own
invitation

設計個人專屬邀請卡

telling someone
they're appreciated
告訴某人，你很感激他

being a hero in little ways
在一些小事上，當個英雄

standing below
a giant tree
站在一棵參天巨樹底下

sending a friend flowers
when they're down
送花給心情不好的朋友

when reality is better
than expectations
事情比預期的更好

doing woodwork
做木工

capturing a small moment on camera
用相機拍下一個瞬間

listening to solid practical advice
傾聽有用的建議

babysitting free for a friend
免費為朋友當保母

choosing your own path
選擇自己的路徑

a team huddle
團隊互擁打氣

laughing at old pictures
of each other
看著彼此的老照片發笑

a well-deserved
vacation
應得的假期

grilling on a summer's day
夏日炙烤

a little alone time every day
每天有一段獨處的時光

leaving all your regrets behind
放下過去一切悔恨

dancing to an old favorite tune
伴著一首喜愛的老歌起舞

*making snow angels*
在雪地上畫出一個完美的天使圖形

*a comfortable silence*
一陣令人舒服的寂靜

*holding a gem to the sun*
把一塊寶石對著陽光

letting the waves tickle your toes
讓浪花輕觸腳趾

that first sip of champagne
on a special occasion
特殊的節日，第一口香檳

having a friend crash on your couch
朋友來你家睡沙發過夜

*a whole day at the beach*
在海濱玩一整天

*drying clothes on the line*
把衣服晾在曬衣繩上

getting ready for a
dress-up party
準備參加化妝舞會

wrapping yourself in a
fuzzy blanket straight
from the dryer
把自己裹進一條
剛烘乾的毛毯裡

sitting on your surfboard
waiting for a wave
坐在沖浪板上，
等待下一個浪頭

seeing big fish from the rocks
站在岸邊岩石上看見大魚

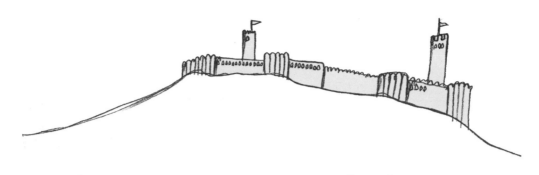

exploring a distant hilltop fort
探索遠方山坡上的城堡

knowing the owner of your local deli
認識了住家附近熟食店的老闆

creating your own language
while traveling
旅行的時候自創一種新語言

walking to work
走路上班

an old-fashioned desk with
lots of secret drawers
一張有很多秘密抽屜的老式書桌

a day at the spa
在水療館度過一天

feeling the breeze
感覺到清風徐來

孤獨漫遊浮若雲，
飄然群山萬壑間

learning a poem by heart
背誦一首詩

researching places for an upcoming trip
為了即將來到的旅遊搜尋景點

water with
cucumber and
lemon
小黃瓜檸檬排毒水

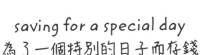

saving for a special day
為了一個特別的日子而存錢

finding a shelf of books in your
language in a foreign bookshop
在國外的書店，看見一整櫃自己母語的圖書

cutting back on
caffeine
咖啡因減量

successfully squeezing
out that last teeny bit
of toothpaste
成功擠出軟管裡
最後一點點牙膏

cracking a joke in a boring meeting
在枯燥的會議上說了個笑話

practicing yo-yo tricks
練習溜溜球的技巧

soaking in a hot spring
泡溫泉

getting lost in a new city
在陌生的城市裡迷路

coming home to a
tidy house

回到整潔的家

biting off the end of the
baguette on your way home

回家路上，咬掉法國長棍麵包的頭

sneaking a note in the lunch box
在午餐盒裡偷偷塞入一張紙條

making friends in the
pool on vacation
渡假時在游泳池認識新朋友

writing a bucket list
寫下一生必做的心願清單

making up stories
編故事

the perfect workout
soundtrack
最適合健身時聆聽的專輯

bugging someone when
they're on the phone
別人講電話的時候去搗蛋

going for a walk
with no destination
漫無目的隨處走

learning to cook
學烹飪

watching a summer storm pass by
看著夏日暴風雨過去

taking off wet shoes
脫掉濕鞋子

sharing secrets
分享小秘密

the reliable sound of
a grandfather clock
老爺鐘發出可靠的聲響

playing in waves
戲水浪花間

*a solo hike*
獨自一人健行

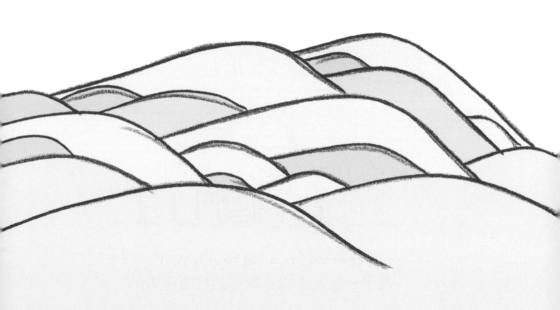

preparing for a big family visit
為了一大家子的人即將到訪而準備

*a horizontalish palm tree*

棕櫚樹的樹幹差點就與地面平行了

a basketful of lovely new yarn
一籃子可愛的新毛線球

an indoor picnic
在家裡辦野餐

a rooftop terrace
屋頂天台

greeting the sunrise
喜迎日出

sampling at an
ice-cream shop
在冰淇淋店試吃

finding a beautiful
feather
找到一根好漂亮的
羽毛

the perfect
power nap
超完美小睡

aromatherapy
芳療

noticing that your kids
have turned out to be
good people

發現孩子長大成為善良的人

rereading your
favorite book

重讀一次最愛的書

a pickup game in the park
在公園裡隨興和別人玩起球來

rolling down a sand dune after a swim
海泳完畢，從沙丘上滾下來

finding a water
fountain when you are
really thirsty

很渴很渴的時候，
找到飲水噴泉

understanding directions given
in a foreign language

對方用外國話告訴你方向，而你聽懂了

when a toddler's laugh
makes you laugh
被幼兒的笑聲逗笑了

catching your dinner
while camping
露營的時候捕獲晚餐

hosting a clothing swap
舉辦一場舊衣交換聚會

mowing the lawn on a beautiful day
利用好天氣割草

when the paper is full of good news
報紙上都是好消息

running with dogs to the park
和狗狗一起用跑的去公園

making someone laugh
把某人逗笑

landing in a new country
降落在一個沒去過的國家

finding your balance
保持平衡

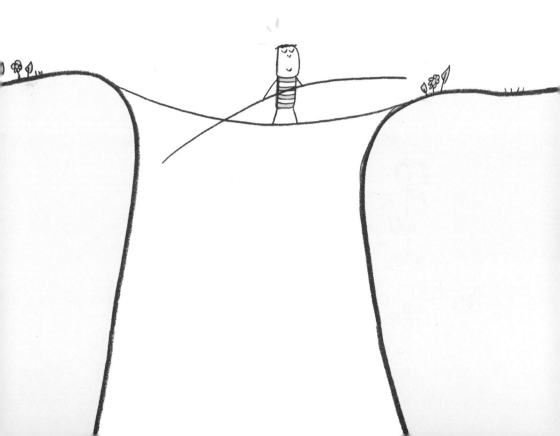

a collection of collections
收藏各式各樣的東西

a camping trip with friends
和朋友來場露營之旅

*a hat with ears on it*
一頂耳朵帽

*a generous helping
when you're really
hungry*

很餓的時候，有一份
超大餐點

*understanding the tides*
瞭解了潮汐

playing Frisbee all afternoon
整個下午都在玩飛盤

a long country drive
在鄉間開了好久的車

takeout on the sofa
在沙發上吃外帶食物

being proud of
yourself
為自己感到驕傲

meeting a friend for an impromptu lunch
和朋友有個重要的午餐約會

just being together

在一起，就好

weekend craft
projects
週末的手作活動

feeling on top of everything
覺得自己超越了一切

a backyard fire
後院升起營火

being patient while standing in line
耐心排隊等待

reading a book in the garden
在庭院裡讀書

a class photo you save forever
一直珍藏的全班合照

exchanging
friendship bracelets
和朋友互換友誼手鍊

getting out the muscle
knots during a massage
按摩時舒緩了緊繃的肌肉

a hot tub in a cold place
在寒冷的地方泡熱水

taking your time to
climb to the top
慢慢爬向頂峰

shouting YEE HAW!
just because
喊著「咿哈！」的歡呼，
沒什麼別的原因

bringing food to a
needy person
為有需要的人帶來食物

rocking a baby
to sleep
成功地把嬰兒搖到睡著

making Popsicles on a hot day
大熱天裡做冰棒

calling your dog for dinner
呼喚狗狗吃晚餐

cooking someone their
favorite meal
為某人烹調他最愛的菜餚

silencing the inner editor
克服了心裡那個惱人的聲音

a picnic on the top of a
mountain
在山頂上野餐

snuggling with a purring cat
和一隻咕嚕的貓依偎在一起

dropping a letter
into the mailbox

把信投入郵筒

touring a new place
with a superb guide
參觀新地方，導覽員好棒

exploring the universe
through a telescope
用望遠鏡探索宇宙

a baby falling
asleep on you
小嬰孩在你身上睡著了

dressing up for no reason
刻意打扮一番，
不為什麼特別的原因

greeting strangers from
the bus window
對著駛過公車裡的陌生人打招呼

*experimenting in the kitchen*
在廚房裡實驗新菜色

Je suis（我是）
Vous êtes（你是）

*speaking a new language*
學一種新的外國語

sharing good news
報好消息

freshly squeezed orange
juice
現榨鮮橙汁

a bird eating from your hand
一隻鳥兒在你手上啄食

sweet solitude
美好的獨處時光

getting something
exciting in the mail
郵筒裡收到令人
興奮的訊息

rocking your bed head
搖晃起床後的頭髮

YES!

saying yes
答應人家

spending time in nature
享受大自然

an unexpected
phone call
一通驚喜的來電

visiting an ancient
place
去訪古蹟

making paper boats and
floating them in a puddle
折好紙船，拿到小水灘去放

daydreaming through the commute
通勤的時候做白日夢

teaching a
child to read
教小朋友閱讀

expressing
yourself
大方表現自己

sitting by a warm heater on
a cold morning
在一個寒冷的早晨，
坐在溫暖的暖爐旁

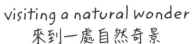

visiting a natural wonder
來到一處自然奇景

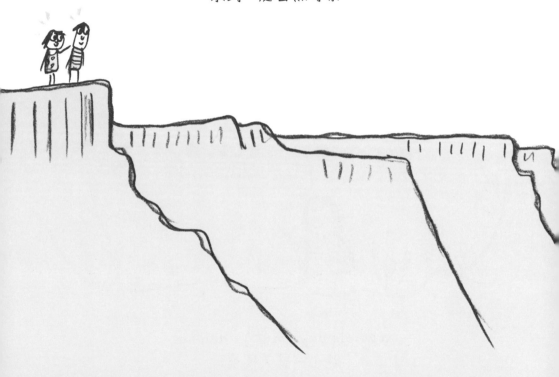

playing a new favorite
track on repeat
反覆播放一首剛喜歡上的樂曲

a whole day spent gardening
做了一整天園藝

watching the flames dance in a fire
看著火焰在營火上跳舞

racing to get back home
比賽誰先到家

playing
make-believe
一場假扮遊戲

making someone smile
when they're sad
某人傷心的時候，逗他發笑

finding a four-leaf clover
找到四葉酢漿草

a day out with a camera
帶著相機出遊

opening a surprise
打開一份驚喜禮物

dropping everything
for a chat
拋下手上的一切，
只為了和人聊天

snuggling under the covers when it's cold
天氣很冷的時候，縮在被子裡

watching the sky from
a hammock
躺在吊床上望著藍天

a friendly feud
君子之爭

pulling a weed out by
its roots
把雜草連根拔起

finding your perfect match
找到絕佳對手

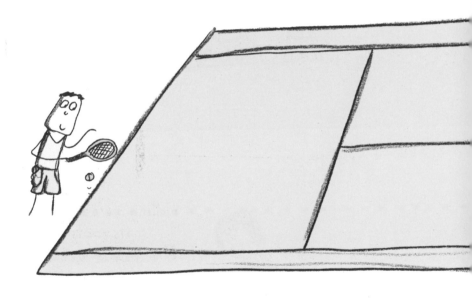

healthy competition
進行良性競爭

telling someone they inspire you
告訴某人，他啟發了你

smiling at a
stranger
對陌生人微笑

*flipping a pancake*
拋鍋讓煎餅翻面

*rubbing your friend's pregnant belly*
摸摸孕婦友人的肚子

*a lazy day with your favorite person*
和你愛的人度過慵懶的一天

turning
cartwheels
倒立

watching whales
賞鯨

cracking the ice
surface on a puddle

踩裂結凍的小水洼

making footprints in fresh snow
在新雪上留下足印

slowly slurping a long noodle
慢慢吸起一條長長的麵條

watching wildlife
欣賞野生動物

complimenting
someone's haircut
誇獎某人的髮型

a candlelit dinner
燭光晚餐

taking a kid for
a shoulder ride
讓孩子跨坐肩頭

sunrise on a mountaintop
山頂上的日出

a morning swim
晨泳

a close game
of cards
比分很接近的牌局

a big warm hug from a
treasured friend
一位值得珍惜的好朋友給我一個
大大的、溫暖的擁抱

doing your small part
to change the world
獻上自己小小的心力
去改變世界

when water sparkles at sunset
落日映照著水面，閃閃發亮

*a giggle fest*
抑不住一直笑一直笑

*waking up to the sound of birds*
在鳥兒鳴叫聲中醒來

going back to the house you grew up in
回到童年成長的老屋

the sound of something
sizzling in the oven
菜餚在烤箱裡滋滋作響

washing your hair with
fabulous-smelling new
shampoo
用一款超級香的洗髮精洗頭

guessing the number of grains
of sand on a beach
猜猜看沙灘上有幾粒沙

266

a night out at
the movies
晚上出去看電影

the smell of chocolate chip
cookies fresh out of the oven
剛烤出來的巧克力脆片餅乾，真香！

telling old family jokes
講一個家族老笑話

a steaming cup of
lemon tea
熱呼呼的檸檬茶

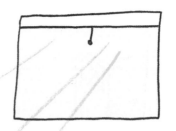

waking up to the sun
shining on your face
醒來時陽光照在臉上

lying in the bath until
your fingers and toes
go all wrinkly
在浴缸裡泡到手指、
腳趾皮膚都起皺

finding a whole
new perspective
發現一個新視角

reading late
into the night
讀書到半夜

*appreciating*
*this moment*
用心體會這個當下

# 快樂就是……
# 500個值得珍惜的當下日常
《快樂就是……》第2集

# happiness is…
# 500 ways to be in the moment

作　　者　麗莎史瓦琳 (Lisa Swerling) ＆拉夫羅拉薩 (Ralph Lazar)
行銷企畫　許凱鈞
責任編輯　陳希林
封面設計　賴姵伶
內文構成　賴姵伶

發 行 人　王榮文
出版發行　遠流出版事業股份有限公司
地　　址　臺北市南昌路2段81號6樓
客服電話　02-2392-6899
傳　　真　02-2392-6658
郵　　撥　0189456-1
著作權顧問　蕭雄淋律師

2018年08月01日　初版一刷
定　　價　平裝新台幣260元（如有缺頁或破損，請寄回更換）
有著作權‧侵害必究　Printed in Taiwan
ISBN　978-957-32-8334-8
遠流博識網　http://www.ylib.com
E-mail：ylib@ylib.com

國家圖書館出版品預行編目(CIP)資料

快樂就是......500個值得珍惜的當下日常 / 麗莎.史瓦琳(Lisa
Swerling), 拉夫.羅拉薩(Ralph Lazar)著；吳齊民譯. -- 初版.
-- 臺北市：遠流, 2018.08
面；　公分
譯自：Happiness is... : 500 ways to be In the moment
ISBN 978-957-32-8334-8(平裝)

1.快樂 2.通俗作品
176.51
107011452